Trivia For Goofy Kids

333 Funny, Silly, Entertaining and Smart Questions That Will Create Hours Upon Hours Of Family Fun!

Jenny Jacobs

Table of Contents

SPECIAL BONUS!

Want These 2 Bonus Books for <u>free</u>?

Get <u>FREE</u>, unlimited access to these and all of our new books by joining the KidsVille Books Facebook group!

PLUS! Get entered into our monthly $20 Amazon Gift card Giveaway

Introduction

Did you know?

Can you guess?

Let me tell you--!

Everyone loves trivia! Whether you're wowing your friends, having a friendly competition with your family, or just want to learn something new, this trivia book is a perfect companion. With over 333 questions in ten different categories, you're sure to find something to catch your eye and keep you reading. Before long, you'll be the one to go to for anyone who wants to know more about the world!

Don't have time to sit and read or find words on paper a bit too overwhelming when your brain is trying to solve trivia puzzles? That's no problem – we also have that issue sometimes! That's why we're offering this book in audio format, too. Play it to yourself before you sleep and wake up with a brain bursting with ideas! It's also a great way to share with large groups because when everyone can hear the questions, it's much harder to peek at the answers.

The important thing is that you use this book how *you* want to and grab as much impressive knowledge as you can. The "how-to" page gives you some hints, but remember, you're the boss! Be creative, now your trivia, and have fun!

Who is this book for?

This book is for kids, teens, and their parents who love a good quiz. What makes trivia so important? Lots of things!

- **Trivia boosts <u>confidence!</u>** It sometimes feels like it's a really hard time to be a kid! It's easy to feel like you're not good enough, not smart enough – but learning trivia and getting questions right helps remind you that's not true at all! Even getting things wrong is good for you; learning to speak out without being afraid is one of the best lessons you can learn with your friends and family.

- **Trivia encourages <u>bonding</u>**: Sometimes it's really tricky to find time and things to do with your family and friends, right? Cracking out this trivia book is a great way to find something you can all do together, no matter your ages or backgrounds. Friendly competition or exciting teamwork will make quiz time fun for everyone!

- **Trivia helps with <u>reading comprehension</u>**: Questions for smart kids and teens means questions with slightly trickier wording than you might be used to! Either reading or listening to these questions will help improve your vocabulary and pronunciation and you'll be able to hold more complicated and clever conversations in no time!

- **Trivia reduces <u>boredom</u>**: There are so many things to do, but it can be hard to find something to fill those quiet moments. Just open your book or press play on your book for a whole world of interesting questions to learn and play with your friends!

- **Trivia makes better <u>concentration</u>**: Concentrating can be hard when there's so many different things going on in the world at any given time. Getting good at trivia means getting good at focusing on just one thing and using all your brainpower for it – something good for adults and kids alike!

What Are Our Categories?

There are ten top trivia categories in total in this book, and they are readable and usable in any order you want. See what tickles your fancy most below!

1	**Movies**	**Are you the one asking for directions, or the one giving them? Use this category to find out who knows their blockbusters or old family favorites!**
2	Music	Okay, so you've proven you know your movies – but can you boogie? Whether you like popular music or not, you're sure to know these songs… Or are you?
3	Sports	The Greeks used to say "a healthy mind lives in a healthy body" and what's better to keep your body healthy than sports?
4	Board Games	The mind needs training too and

8	Disney	Even adults include Disney in their quizzes because there's just so much in every Disney movie! Everyone has their favorite, and if you're a fan, you'll be able to rattle off enough answers to make your friends' heads spin.
9	Theme Parks	Amuse yourself with fun facts from theme parks all over the world! Are you a thrill seeker or go there for the food? Do you know what's the oldest theme park in the world? Test your thrilling knowledge here!
10	Tv Shows	TV shows can be so much more satisfying than movies because you get to stay with beloved characters for so much longer! The last category in this book is sure to refresh some of your favorite people from the small screen!

How to Use This Book

The most important rule is to have fun with it. The rest is up to you! Here are the pain points if you're a bit puzzled about where to get started.

- Each chapter has thirty-three questions about one of the categories mentioned above. (With some surprises in the end!)
- You can read the chapters in any order!
- Each multiple-choice question has an answer either at the end of the chapter or after an audio pause.
- Challenge your friends and family or simply read alone to gather as much info as possible. Who'll be crowned the trivia monarch?
- You can use the audio version in the car or over dinner, and you can have your book on you wherever you go! Look for opportunities to use it with everyone.

Some dos and don'ts.

Do

- ✓ Revisit old questions after a while – see what you can remember
- ✓ Get other people involved. Trivia is fun in groups!

✓ Let people know the right answer if they get it wrong!

Don't

- Cheat – what's the point in trivia if you're just going to look up the answer before even guessing?
- Ruin it for everyone – if you've already read the answer or done this question before, let someone else have a go!
- Brag – Winning is great, but remember it's supposed to be fun, too!

Category 1: Movies

1. In "Ice Age: Continental Drift", Manny, Sid, and Diego are trapped on what?

a) A Raft
b) An Ice Block
c) A Mountain
d) A Tree

Answer: Pg. 25

2. In "The Lorax", what color is the Lorax?

a) Pink
b) Blue
c) Orange
d) Purple

Answer: Pg. 25

3. In "The Incredibles" what superpower does Violet have?

a) Flight

b) Invisibility
c) Super Strength
d) Super Speed

Answer: Pg. 25

4. In the movie 'Peter Pan' who is Captain Hook's pirate-buddy?

a) Pan
b) Tink
c) The Big Chief
d) Smee

Answer: Pg. 25

5. What is the name of Woody's horse in "Toy Story 2"?

a) Bullseye
b) Desperado
c) Andy
d) Buzz

Answer: Pg. 25

6. In the movie 'ET' what does Elliot dress up ET as for Halloween?

a) a ghost with boots
b) a ghost with clown feet
c) a ghost with a bike
d) a ghost with no feet

Answer: Pg. 25

7. In the movie "Monsters, Inc.", who is big and tall with blue fur and purple spots?

a) Mike
b) Randall
c) Sulley
d) Boo

Answer: Pg. 25

8. Who is Wreck-It Ralph's enemy in "Wreck-It Ralph"?

a) Fix-It Felix, Jr.
b) Sonic the Hedgehog
c) Fix-It Ralph Jr.
d) Super Mario

Answer: Pg. 25

9. In the movie 'Annie' what is Annie's dog's name?

a) Lady
b) Marlin
c) Roger
d) Sandy

Answer: Pg. 25

10. What are the names of Ella's stepsisters in the film "Ella Enchanted"?

a) Hattie and Mattie
b) Lisa and Mary
c) Hattie And Olive
d) Emma and Ruby

Answer: Pg. 25

11. In "The NeverEnding Story" what kind of creature is Falkor?

a) A Luck Dragon
b) A Giant Hawk
c) A centaur
d) A Gnome

Answer: Pg. 25

12. What Dreamworks movie features a snooty pet mouse who ends up in the sewers?

a) Rango
b) Flushed Away
c) Bolt
d) Stuart Little

Answer: Pg. 25

13. What are the little people called in "Charlie and the Chocolate Factory"?

a) Fidgets
b) Ridgets
c) Loompa Toombas
d) Oompa Loompas

Answer: Pg. 25

14. What was a scenario featured in "Despicable Me"?

a) A villain and his sidekick try to steal the moon by using a shrink-ray.
b) A villain and his sidekick move to the moon and attempt to use a shrink-ray on Earth

c)   A sentient statue declares war against all pigeons
d)   An alien decides to go on a date

Answer: Pg. 25

15. In "Happy Feet", who is the penguin who can't sing?

a)   Thimble
b)   Rumble
c)   Temple
d)   Mumble

Answer: Pg. 25

16. In "The Lion, the Witch and the Wardrobe", what is the first thing Lucy sees when she enters the forest?

a)   A horse carriage
b)   A map of Narnia
c)   A lamppost
d)   A lion

Answer: Pg. 25

17. In which movie did Antonio Banderas play Gregorio Cortez?

a) The Road to El Dorado
b) Atlantis
c) Spy Kids
d) Sharkboy and Lavagirl

Answer: Pg. 25

18. What type of animal was Marty in the movie "Madagascar"?

a) Toucan
b) Hippo
c) Lion
d) Zebra

Answer: Pg. 25

19. Where did the Grinch steal Christmas?

a) Whoville
b) Whereville
c) Whichville
d) Whatville

Answer: Pg. 25

20. In "Alvin and the Chipmunks" which chipmunk has nightmares and gets in bed with Dave?

a) Alvin
b) Theodore
c) Simon
d) Eleanor

Answer: Pg. 25

21. In "The Dark Crystal", what does Kira say about prophets?

a) They Don't Know Everything
b) They Don't Know Who I Am
c) They Know Nothing
d) They Know Everything

Answer: Pg. 25

22. In "Land Before Time II" who did Littlefoot and his friends see a lot?

a) Rex
b) Gnawer
c) Chomper
d) Biter

Answer: Pg. 25

23. In the Lego Movie, Unikitty is the princess of…?

a) Far Far Away Land
b) Everything
c) The World
d) Cloud Cuckoo Land

Answer: Pg. 25

24. What animated movie features Watch, Madame Gasket and Cappy?

a) Wall-E
b) Robots
c) Toy Story
d) Bee Movie

Answer: Pg. 25

25. In "How to Train Your Dragon", Hiccup loses what body part?

a) His left foot
b) His right foot
c) His left arm
d) His right foot

26. What was the name of Dorothy's dog in the Wizard of Oz?

    a) Oz
    b) Titus
    c) Africa
    d) Toto

Answer: Pg. 25

27. In "Bridge to Terabithia", at which sport was Jesse trying to beat the other boys?

    a) Baseball
    b) Running
    c) Football
    d) Swimming

Answer: Pg. 26

28. In the movie Polar Express, where does the young boy travel to by train?

    a) Sweden
    b) The South Pole

c)   The North Pole
d)   Finland

Answer: Pg. 26

29. What does Paddington Bear keep underneath his hat in case of emergency?

a)   A pot of honey
b)   A jar of bees
c)   A pillow
d)   A Marmalade Sandwich

Answer: Pg. 26

30. What movie is based on a singing competition between a mouse, a pig, a gorilla, and elephant, and a porcupine?

a)   Happy Feet
b)   Sing
c)   Over the Hedge
d)   Frozen

Answer: Pg. 26

31. What are the names of the kids in the "Spy Kids" movies?

a) Maria and Esteban
b) Juan and Carla
c) Juanita and Santiago
d) Carmen and Juni

Answer: Pg. 26

32. What are the names of the three blue birds from the Angry
Birds movies?

a) Jay, Jake and Jim
b) Sam, Jam, and Slam
c) Ed, Ned, and Eddy
d) Joseph, Jimko, and Johnny

Answer: Pg. 26

33. In Captain Underpants: The First Epic Movie" Melvin's nanny
cam was disguised as this animal.

a) Penguin
b) Turtle
c) Bear
d) Dog

Answer: Pg. 26

Category 1: Answers

Question	Letter	Answer
1	B	An Ice block
2	C	The Lorax is orange
3	B	Violet can turn invisible
4	D	Smee is Captain Hook's assistant
5	A	Woody's trusty horse is named Bullseye
6	B	He dresses up as a ghost with clown feet
7	C	James *P. "Sulley" Sullivan, one of the main characters*
8	A	Fix-It Felix, Jr.
9	D	She names the dog Sandy because it's the color of sand
10	C	They're named Hattie And Olive
11	A	He is a Luck Dragon
12	B	Flushed away. The mouse is flushed accidentally in the sewers
13	D	The Oompa-Loompas
14	A	A villain and his sidekick try to steal the moon by using a shrink-ray.
15	D	Mumble
16	C	A lamppost
17	C	The Spy Kids movies
18	D	He was a Zebra
19	A	Whoville
20	B	Theodore
21	A	"They Don't Know Everything"
22	C	Chomper
23	D	Cloud Cuckoo Land
24	B	Robots
25	A	He loses his left foot
26	D	The dog's name is Toto.

27	B	Running
28	C	The North Pole
29	D	A marmalade sandwich
30	B	Sing
31	D	Carmen and Juni
32	A	Jay, Jake and Jim
33	B	The nanny cam was a turtle toy

Category 2: Music

1. "Spring Day" is the title track off which BTS album?

    a)   Youth
    b)   Dark & Wild
    c)   You Never Walk Alone
    d)   Wings

Answer: Pg. 39

2. What is Ariana Grande's real full name?

    a)   Ariana Smith
    b)   Ariana Venti
    c)   Ariana Grande-Broccoli
    d)   Ariana Grande-Butera

Answer: Pg. 39

3. What is the opening line to Queen's song 'Bohemian Rhapsody'?

    a)   Is this the real life? Is this just fantasy?

b) I see a little silhouetto of a man! Scaramouche, Scaramouche, will you do the Fandango?
c) Is this my real life or just my fantasy?
d) Is it a real knife?

Answer: Pg. 39

4. What does Despacito mean?

a) Quietly
b) Slowly
c) Little woman
d) Little dance

Answer: Pg. 39

5. Which band does Halsey shout out in 'Closer'?

a) Fall Out Boy
b) Panic! At the Disco
c) Blink-182
d) My Chemical Romance

Answer: Pg. 39

6. What is Daddy Yankee's real name?

a) Luis Santiago Ramos
b) Daddy Yankee is his real name
c) Juan Antonio de la Fuente
d) Ramón Luis Ayala Rodríguez

Answer: Pg. 39

7. Which of these songs spent the most weeks on top of the Hot 100?

a) Luis Fonsi& Daddy Yankee - 'Despacito'
b) Calvin Harris & Rag'n'bone Man – 'Giant'
c) Lil Nas X & Billy Ray Cyrus - 'Old Town Road'-
d) Ed Sheeran - 'Shape of You'

Answer: Pg. 39

8. The name Imagine Dragons is in fact an anagram. What is it an anagram of?

a) AM Ginseng Radio
b) Agonising Dream
c) Dagger Insomnia
d) Only the members of the band know

Answer: Pg. 39

9. Beebo, the puppet that shares likeness with Panic! at the Disco's frontman Brendon Urie wears a fabulous sequin jacket. What color is it?

   a) Red
   b) Silver
   c) Gold
   d) Blue

Answer: Pg. 39

10. Which Grammy Award did 21 Pilots accept in their underwear?

   a) Best Alternative Music Album
   b) Best Rock Performance
   c) Record of the Year
   d) Best Pop Duo/Group Performance

Answer: Pg. 39

11. What classic rock band's members used the name of the band as their last names?

   a) The Ramones
   b) The Doors
   c) The Who
   d) Rainbow

Answer: Pg. 39

12. What song was the first YouTube video to be viewed 1 billion times?

    a)   Without Me by Eminem
    b)   Toxic by Britney Spears
    c)   Despacito by Luis Fonsi& Daddy Yankee
    d)   Gangnam Style by PSY

Answer: Pg. 39

13. Maroon 5 claimed to have 'the moves like' which member of the Rolling Stones?

    a)   (Keith) Richards
    b)   (Mick) Jagger
    c)   (Charlie) Watts
    d)   (Ronnie) Wood

Answer: Pg. 39

14. In which year did Little Mix win The X Factor?

    a)   2011

b) 2010
c) 2012
d) 2014

Answer: Pg. 39

15. What is the name of Miley Cyrus' father?

a) Robby Ray Cyrus
b) Billy Jay Cyrus
c) Billy Ray Cyrus
d) Bobby Ray Cyrus

Answer: Pg. 39

16. What does 'Karaoke' mean?

a) Empty Orchestra
b) Empty Lyrics
c) Singing Contest
d) Singing Lyrics

Answer: Pg. 39

17. Who was the most streamed artist on Spotify in 2019?

a) Rihanna
b) Lil Nas X
c) J Balvin
d) Ed Sheeran

Answer: Pg. 39

18. "Con Calma" by Puerto Rican rapper Daddy Yankee is a reimagination of which song by the Canadian rapper Snow?

a) "Boom Boom Boogie"
b) "Nothin' on Me"
c) "Adore You"
d) "Informer"

Answer: Pg. 39

19. What is Hozier's real name?

a) Andy Wright-Hozier
b) Adam Hozier-Bright
c) Andrew Hozier-Byrne
d) Anthony Blue Ryan

Answer: Pg. 39

20. The oldest known musical instruments in the world are
between 42,000 and 43,000 years old, what are they?

    a) Drums
    b) Flutes
    c) Bagpipes
    d) Tambourines

Answer: Pg. 39

21. Who won a People's Choice Award for Favorite Pop Artist in
2012?

    a) Miley Cyrus
    b) Katy Perry
    c) Demi Lovato
    d) Taylor Swift

Answer: Pg. 39

22. Selena Gomez had an organ transplant? What was it?

    a) Kidney
    b) Heart
    c) Bone marrow
    d) Liver

Answer: Pg. 39

23. In what year did Lizzo release 'Truth Hurts'?

    a) 2018
    b) 2016
    c) 2019
    d) 2017

Answer: Pg. 40

24. Billie Eilish's debut album was called "When We All ______,
Where Do We Go?"

    a) Dissociate
    b) Fall Asleep
    c) Pass Out
    d) Die

Answer: Pg. 40

25. How old was Adele when she released 25?

    a) 27
    b) 26
    c) 25
    d) 24

Answer: Pg. 40

26. What is Halsey's real name?

    a)   Ashley Nicolette Frangipane
    b)   Aline Green Montenegro
    c)   Carmen Nicole Oliveira
    d)   Alba Sophia Flores

Answer: Pg. 40

27. Post Malone has a face tattoo that reads what below his eyes?

    a)   No Regrets
    b)   Always Winning
    c)   Always Tired
    d)   Self-Made

Answer: Pg. 40

28. What instrument did Lil Nas X play in Grade school?

    a)   Cello
    b)   Trumpet

c) Violin
d) Trombone

Answer: Pg. 40

29. Who sings the credits version of "Into the Unknown" in Disney's Frozen 2?

a) Panic! At the Disco
b) Fall Out Boy
c) My Chemical Romance
d) Ed Sheeran

Answer: Pg. 40

30. Who is the first woman in the history of the Billboard Hot 100 to have three simultaneous top 10 singles as a lead artist?

a) Miley Cyrus
b) Mariah Carey
c) Adele
d) Billie Eilish

Answer: Pg. 40

31. The Jonas Brothers and Selena Gomez both scored their Number 1s in 2019 with what song?

a) "Sucker"
b) "Cool"
c) "Only Human"
d) "Like It's Christmas"

Answer: Pg. 40

32. What famous rapper interrupted Taylor Swift's speech at the 2009 VMA's?

a) Eminem
b) Kanye West
c) Lil Nas X
d) Snoop Dog

Answer: Pg. 40

33. Which One Direction member sings "Sign of the Times"?

a) Harry Styles
b) Liam Payne
c) Louis Tomlinson
d) Zayn Malik

Answer: Pg. 40

Category 2: Answers

Question	Letter	Answer
1	C	You Never Walk Alone
2	D	Ariana Grande-Butera
3	A	Is this the real life? Is this just fantasy?
4	B	It means slowly, unhurriedly.
5	C	Halsey sings 'Stay and play that blink-182 song'.
6	D	Ramón Luis Ayala Rodríguez
7	C	'Old Town Road' was in the US charts for a record-breaking 19 weeks
8	D	No one knows apart from the band members.
9	C	His jacket is gold
10	D	Best Pop Duo/Group Performance
11	A	The Ramones
12	D	On 21 December 2012, "Gangnam Style" became the first YouTube video to reach one billion views.
13	B	Maroon 5 have the moves like Jagger
14	A	2011
15	C	His name is Billy Ray Cyrus
16	A	The word karaoke comes from the Japanese words 'kara' meaning 'empty' and 'oke' meaning 'orchestra'.
17	D	Ed Sheeran
18	D	Snow's 1992 single "Informer"
19	C	Andrew Hozier-Byrne
20	B	Flutes
21	C	Demi Lovato
22	A	She had a kidney transplant. Her best friend donated the kidney.
23	D	Lizzo released 'Truth Hurts' in 2017 but

		it didn't go Number 1 in the US until 2019.
24	B	Fall Asleep
25	A	27. Adele wrote and recorded the majority of 25 when she was 25. However, she didn't release the album until she was 27.
26	A	Ashley Nicolette Frangipane
27	C	Post Malone has a face tattoo that reads 'Always Tired' below his eyes.
28	B	He played the trumpet
29	A	Panic! At the Disco
30	C	Adele
31	A	The band released their first single in nearly five years, "Sucker", which topped the *Billboard* Hot 100.
32	B	Kanye West interrupted Taylor Swift's speech which spawned the "I'mma let you finish" internet meme
33	A	Harry Styles

Category 3: Sports

1. Who is the fastest man in the world at 100-meter sprint as of 2016?

   a)   Usain Bolt
   b)   Andre De Grasse
   c)   Justin Gatlin
   d)   Wayde van Niekerk

Answer: Pg. 53

2. How many athletic events are in a decathlon?

   a)   12
   b)   10
   c)   13
   d)   8

Answer: Pg. 53

3. How many players are there in a cricket team on the field?

   a)   12

b) 10
c) 8
d) 11

Answer: Pg. 53

4. Which country invented the game baseball?

a) England
b) USA
c) Australia
d) Ireland

Answer: Pg. 53

5. What is the name of the racquet game played in a closed wall court?

a) Tennis
b) Badminton
c) Squash
d) Speedball

Answer: Pg. 53

6. What is Zumba?

a) A ball sport
b) A pool sport
c) A racket sport
d) A dance cardio workout

Answer: Pg. 53

7. How many red balls are on the table at the beginning of a game of snooker?

a) 3
b) 1
c) 15
d) 20

Answer: Pg. 53

8. How many rings form the Olympic logo?

a) Seven
b) Five
c) Eight
d) Six

Answer: Pg. 53

9. Which sport uses the lightest ball?

    a)   Volleyball
    b)   Table tennis
    c)   Water Polo
    d)   Football

Answer: Pg. 53

10. In what game is the word 'love' used?

    a)   Tennis
    b)   Softball
    c)   Racquetball
    d)   Ping Pong

Answer: Pg. 53

11. What type of race is the Tour de France?

    a)   A marathon
    b)   A boat race
    c)   A bicycle race
    d)   A car race

Answer: Pg. 53

12. What are the colors of the five Olympic rings?

    a) Orange, yellow, green, blue and black
    b) Gold, yellow, green, blue and black
    c) Red, yellow, purple, blue and black
    d) Red, yellow, green, blue and black

Answer: Pg. 53

13. How often is the football world cup held?

    a) Every 4 years
    b) Every year
    c) Every 2 years
    d) Every 10 years

Answer: Pg. 53

14. In which country is it tradition for rugby teams to perform a war dance known as the haka before a match begins?

    a) France
    b) Australia
    c) New Zealand
    d) England

Answer: Pg. 53

15. How many players are there in a rugby league team?

    a) 13
    b) 14
    c) 12
    d) 11

Answer: Pg. 53

16. Which three sports form a triathlon?

    a) Boxing, wrestling, and climbing
    b) Swimming, cycling and running
    c) Swimming, climbing, and Jumping
    d) Jumping, weight lifting, and running

Answer: Pg. 53

17. How many players are in an ice hockey team?

    a) 5
    b) 4
    c) 6
    d) 7

Answer: Pg. 53

18. Which flag is waved in motor racing to show the winner?

  a) A red and white checkered flag
  b) A black and red checkered flag
  c) A black and white checkered flag
  d) A red and white checkered flag

Answer: Pg. 53

19. Which country invented Volleyball?

  a) Australia
  b) Spain
  c) France
  d) The United States of America

Answer: Pg. 53

20. What type of sport is the name Mo Farah associated with?

  a) Running
  b) Swimming
  c) Climbing
  d) Wrestling

Answer: Pg. 53

21. Ice hockey uses a rubber disc called what?

    a)   Ducky
    b)   Puck
    c)   Sticky
    d)   Rook

Answer: Pg. 53

22. What is the highest possible score to get in a game of darts when using three darts?

    a)   160
    b)   120
    c)   130
    d)   180

Answer: Pg. 53

23. How many holes are there in a bowling ball used in tenpin bowling?

    a)   2

b) 5
c) 3
d) 4

Answer: Pg. 53

24. In which sport can you score a bullseye?

a) Darts
b) Fencing
c) Water Polo
d) Rodeo

Answer: Pg. 53

25. What color is the center of the target in archery?

a) Red
b) Black
c) White
d) Gold

Answer: Pg. 53

26. Which chess piece holds the most value on a chess board?

a) The Queen
b) The King
c) The Bishop
d) The Knight

Answer: Pg. 53

27. What city hosts the Wimbledon Tennis Championships?

a) Dublin
b) Belfast
c) Edinburgh
d) London

Answer: Pg. 53

28. How many pockets are there on a snooker table?

a) 8
b) 10
c) 4
d) 6

Answer: Pg. 54

29. What sport is Michael Phelps associated with?

a) Running
b) Soccer
c) Swimming
d) Climbing

Answer: Pg. 54

30. The first Olympic Games took place in Olympia, Greece. What century was that?

a) 8th century B.C.
b) 5th century B.C.
c) 3th century B.C.
d) 7th century B.C.

Answer: Pg. 54

31. Which American woman has the most Olympic medals for swimming?

a) Dara Torres
b) Natalie Coughlin
c) Jenny Thompson
d) Katie Ledecky

Answer: Pg. 54

32. Who of these women is a javelin athlete?

    a)   Mirela Maniani
    b)   Tianna Madison
    c)   Elmira Alembekova
    d)   Iolanda Balaş

Answer: Pg. 54

33. What are **Irish stepdance competitions called?**

    a)   Soshanna
    b)   Feiseanna
    c)   Arshanna
    d)   Mashanna

Answer: Pg. 54

Category 3: Answers

Question	Letter	Answer
1	A	Usain Bolt
2	B	10. Deka means ten in Greek, decathlon literally meaning ten sports.
3	D	11
4	A	England
5	C	Squash
6	D	Zumba is dance workout invented by Beto Perez.
7	C	Fifteen
8	B	Five to represent unity.
9	B	Table Tennis.
10	A	Tennis
11	C	Bicycle Race
12	D	Red, yellow, green, blue and black
13	A	Every four years
14	C	New Zealand
15	A	Thirteen
16	B	Swimming, cycling, and running
17	C	Six
18	C	Black and white checkered flag
19	D	The USA
20	A	Running
21	B	Puck
22	D	180 points
23	C	Three
24	A	Darts!
25	D	Gold but the bullseye is sometimes black
26	A	The Queen
27	D	London, England

28	D	Six
29	C	Swimming, he has 28 Olympic medals
30	A	8th Century BC
31	C	Jenny Thompson, she has 12 Olympic medals
32	A	Mirella Maniani
33	B	Feiseanna

Category 4: Board Games

1. People think Monopoly the board game was invented by Charles Darrow in 1933 but who was the actual inventor?

   a) Elizabeth Magie
   b) The Parker Brothers
   c) James Darrow
   d) J.P. Morgan

Answer: Pg. 67

2. Over the years, Uno has created several themed packs of the game. Which one of these was a themed pack?

   a) Disney Characters
   b) Barbie
   c) Super Heroes
   d) All of the above

Answer: Pg. 67

3. In Trivial Pursuit, questions are split into six categories each with its own color. Literature was originally brown, what was the color used later?

a) Green
b) Purple
c) Yellow
d) Orange

Answer: Pg. 67

4. In Candyland, what is the name of the lady who lives in the peanut brittle house?

a) Peanut Butter
b) Ms. Hazel Nutt
c) Gramma Nutt
d) Ms. Pecan

Answer: Pg. 67

5. In the Game of Life, how much money do stocks cost?

a) $50,000
b) $150,000
c) $20,000
d) $100,000

Answer: Pg. 67

6. Skydivers played this game during a 13,000-foot drop.

a) Chess
b) Scrabble
c) Monopoly
d) Checkers

Answer: Pg. 67

7. A checkers board has been dated to 3,000 B.C. Where was it uncovered?

a) Peru
b) Iran
c) Iraq
d) Egypt

Answer: Pg. 67

8. Which of these weapons does not exist in standard Clue?

a) The Shovel
b) The Lead Pipe
c) The revolver
d) The Candlestick

Answer

9. How big are the blocks in the world's largest Jenga?

    a) 9'
    b) 8'
    c) 10'
    d) 7'

Answer: Pg. 67

10 Scrabble tournaments use special tiles. What is special about them?

    a) They glow in the dark
    b) They are red
    c) They are worth half the points
    d) They are smooth

Answer: Pg. 67

11. In "Operation", what is the name of the character that is undergoing the operation?

    a) Cavity Sam
    b) Yosemite Sam
    c) John Doe
    d) Patient X

Answer: Pg. 67

12. Which board game became the first non-coffee related product that Starbucks ever sold?

   a) Risk
   b) Trivial Pursuit
   c) Pictionary
   d) Cranium

Answer: Pg. 67

13. Fidel Castro banned this board game.

   a) Risk
   b) Monopoly
   c) Life
   d) Battleship

Answer: Pg. 67

14. What does the word 'Jenga' mean in Swahili?

   a) To topple
   b) To assemble
   c) To build
   d) To tip

Answer: Pg. 68

15. In Candyland, what is the name of the guy next to the candy cane space on the board?

    a) Mr. Mint
    b) Mr. Stripes
    c) Mr. Cane
    d) Mr. Candy

Answer: Pg. 68

16. What country is Trivial Pursuit from?

    a) France
    b) Canada
    c) USA
    d) Belgium

Answer: Pg. 68

17. Which game was inspired by Rube Goldberg?

    a) Risk
    b) Connect 4

c) Mouse Trap
d) Clue

Answer: Pg. 68

18. Who is the dead heiress in 13 Dead End Drive?

a) Aunt Agatha
b) Aunt Mab
c) Aunt Delores
d) Aunt Beatrice

Answer: Pg. 68

19. How many female characters appear in the original Guess Who?

a) Fourteen
b) Ten
c) Five
d) Thirteen

Answer: Pg. 68

20. What is checkers called in England?

a) Drats
b) Drafts
c) Drawers
d) Draughts

Answer: Pg. 68

21. Which game's first 5,000 copies sold out too fast even for its inventor?

a) Uno
b) Risk
c) Trivial Pursuit
d) Settlers of Catan

Answer: Pg. 68

22. What color peg indicates a hit in Battleship?

a) Yellow
b) Red
c) Orange
d) Black

Answer: Pg. 68

23. What classic game was once referred to as "tables"?

a) Backgammon
b) Chess
c) Checkers
d) Reversi

Answer: Pg. 68

24. Which is not a possible career in the Game of Life?

a) Athlete
b) Artist
c) Lawyer
d) Doctor

Answer: Pg. 68

25. How much does the most expensive set of Monopoly cost?

a) $3 million
b) $2 million
c) $10 million
d) $1 million

Answer: Pg. 68

26. What game was originally called La Conqueste du Monde?

64

a) Risk
b) Settlers of Catan
c) Battleship
d) Othello

Answer: Pg. 68

27. What is the actual name for the castle piece in chess?

a) Castle
b) Bishop
c) Knight
d) Rook

Answer: Pg. 68

28. UNO cards in the colors of.

a) White, yellow, blue, and red
b) Purple, orange, green, and red
c) Green, yellow, blue, and red
d) Purple, yellow, green, and red

Answer: Pg. 68

29. Who is the youngest female suspect in Clue?

   a) Miss Peach
   b) Mrs. White
   c) Miss Scarlett
   d) Mrs. Peacock

Answer: Pg. 68

30. What is the traditional name for the game Othello?

   a) Reversi
   b) Bantumi
   c) Iago
   d) Cassio

Answer: Pg. 68

31. What board game is a simplified version of Capture the Flag?

   a) Stratego
   b) Backgammon
   c) Settlers of Catan
   d) Risk

Answer: Pg. 68

32. How many ships do players get in Battleship?

    a) Three
    b) Seven
    c) Four
    d) Five

Answer: Pg. 68

33. How many balls should Hungry Hungry Hippos have?

    a) 10
    b) 20
    c) 18
    d) 16

Answer: Pg. 68

Category 4: Answers

Question	Letter	Answer
1	A	Elizabeth 'Lizzie' Magie. She invented The Landlord's Game, the precursor to Monopoly but Charles Darrow claimed the idea as his own.
2	D	All of the above
3	B	Literature& Arts was changed to purple
4	C	Her name is Gramma Nutt
5	A	$50,000
6	B	They played Scrabble
7	C	It was uncovered during a dig in the Sumerian city-state of Ur, that is now located in Iraq
8	A	The Shovel
9	B	Caterpillar Inc. used five of its construction vehicles to play a super game of Jenga. The solid pine blocks were 8 feet long, 32 times the length of a standard Jenga block.
10	D	They are smooth. Traditional Scrabble sets come with wooden tiles with grooved letters, these tiles aren't used in high-level tournaments as players have been caught cheating by touch.
11	A	His name is Cavity Sam
12	D	It was the board game Cranium
13	B	Fidel Castro banned all versions of Monopoly, including a Cuban knockoff called "Capitolio" that features the streets of Havana.
14	C	The name Jenga is based on the Swahili word that means "to build.

15	A	His name is Mr. Mint
16	B	Trivial Pursuit is Canadian
17	C	Mousetrap was inspired by Rube Goldberg's devices
18	A	Aunt Agatha
19	C	Only five
20	D	Checkers is called Draughts in England.
21	D	The first 5,000 copies of Settlers of Catan sold out so fast that its inventor Klaus Teuber doesn't have the first edition copy.
22	B	Red pegs indicate hits
23	A	Backgammon was known as tables and may date back to 300 C.E.
24	C	Lawyer
25	B	A San Francisco jeweler made an extremely luxe version of Monopoly in 1988. He created a $2 million Monopoly set that included a gold board, and diamond-encrusted dice
26	A	Risk. La Conqueste du Monde means "The World's Conquest"
27	D	It's called a Rook
28	C	UNO cards are green, yellow, blue and red.
29	C	Miss Scarlett is the youngest
30	A	Reversi
31	A	Stratego. The objective is to find and capture the opponent's Flag, or to capture so many enemy pieces that the opponent has to forfeit.
32	D	Five ships
33	B	20 balls

Category 5: Star Adventures

1. In "Star Wars: The Last Jedi", what does Benicio Del Toro's character "DJ" stand for?

    a) Doe John
    b) Don Juan
    c) Dark Jedi
    d) Don't Join

Answer: Pg. 81

2. Which actor is the only one who's appeared in every single "Star Wars" movie to date?

    a) Anthony Daniels
    b) Mark Hamill
    c) Carrie Fisher
    d) Harrison Ford

Answer: Pg. 81

3. Where did the Clone Wars begin?

    a) Naboo

b) Tatooine
c) Geonosis
d) Coruscant

Answer: Pg. 81

4. According to the Emperor, what was Luke Skywalker's weakness?

a) His faith in Obi Wan
b) His faith in his friends
c) His lack of training
d) His bad lightsaber technique

Answer: Pg. 81

5. What is the first word of the opening crawl of The Force Awakens?

a) War
b) Luke
c) Darth
d) Stormtroopers

Answer: Pg. 81

6. Who originally stole the Millennium Falcon from Han Solo?

a) Jango Fett
b) Kylo Ren
c) Ducain
d) Maz Kanata

Answer: Pg. 81

7. What happened to Anakin Skywalker during the battle with Count Dooku?

a) He lost his legs
b) He lost his right arm
c) He lost his sight
d) He died

Answer: Pg. 81

8. Who adopted Padmé Amidala's daughter?

a) Bail Organa
b) Boba Fett
c) Owen and Beru Lars
d) Count Dooku

Answer: Pg. 81

9. What are Leia's final words to Han?

   a)   "I love you."
   b)   "May the Force be with you."
   c)   "If you see our son, bring him home."
   d)   "No matter how much we fought, I've always hated
        watching you leave."

Answer: Pg. 81

10. Which famous actor did **NOT** have a cameo in The Force
Awakens?

   a)   Simon Pegg
   b)   Daniel Craig
   c)   Tom Hardy
   d)   Billie Lourde

Answer: Pg. 81

11. What is the name of General Leia Organa's ship?

   a)   Raddus
   b)   Virago
   c)   Millennium Falcon
   d)   Radian VI

Answer: Pg. 81

12. What are the massive horse-like creatures on Canto Bight called?

   a)   Caretakers
   b)   Fathiers
   c)   Porgs
   d)   Vulptices

Answer: Pg. 81

13. What is Poe Dameron's callsign?

   a)   Black Spider
   b)   Green Spider
   c)   Black Leader
   d)   Green Leader

Answer: Pg. 81

14. Where does Rey live on the planet of Jakku?

   a)   in the remains of an Imperial Destroyer
   b)   in the remains of an AT-AT
   c)   in a cave
   d)   With General Organa

15. How many guards are in Supreme Leader Snoke's Elite Praetorian Guard?

    a) Two
    b) Six
    c) Four
    d) Eight

Answer: Pg. 81

16. Which of the following is **NOT** a Maz Kanata quote?

    a) "We all need to fight."
    b) "I'm looking at the eyes of a man who wants to run."
    c) "Where's my boyfriend?"
    d) "I know the Force."

Answer: Pg. 81

17. What is Finn's real name?

    a) FN-2187
    b) FN-8712

c)   FN-8127
d)   FN-7812

Answer: Pg. 81

18. What system did the First Order's Starkiller base destroy in The Force Awakens?

a)   Yavin
b)   Takodana
c)   Bespin
d)   Hosnian

Answer: Pg. 81

19. Which actor did **NOT** make a cameo in The Last Jedi?

a)   Justin Theroux
b)   Tom Hardy
c)   Daniel Radcliffe
d)   Joseph Gordon-Levitt

Answer: Pg. 81

20. Who Erased Kamino from the Jedi-Archives?

a)   Count Dooku
b)   Darth Sidious
c)   Sifo-Dyas
d)   Darth Vader

Answer: Pg. 81

21. Who killed Jabba?

a)   Han Solo
b)   Princess Leia
c)   C-3PO
d)   Luke Skywalker

Answer: Pg. 81

22. Finn worked for which department on the Starkiller Base?

a)   Medical
b)   Engineering
c)   Sanitation
d)   Human resources

Answer: Pg. 81

23. What giant pig creature does Finn share a drink with on Jakku?

a) Wampa
b) Happabore
c) Anooba
d) Jakrab

Answer: Pg. 81

24. What's the name of "Broom Boy" in the final scene of The Last Jedi?

a) C'ai Threnalli
b) Koo Millham
c) Paige Tico
d) Temiri Blegg

Answer: Pg. 81

25. What is the name of the First Order's "Gorilla Walkers"?

a) AT-AP
b) AT-M6
c) OG-9
d) AT-ACT

Answer: Pg. 81

26. How many portions does Unkar Plutt offer for BB-8?

    a) None
    b) 6
    c) 60
    d) 6,000

Answer: Pg. 81

27. Which planet is Luke Skywalker on in The Force Awakens?

    a) Ahch-To
    b) Tatooine
    c) Scarif
    d) Jakku

Answer: Pg. 81

28. Which actor/director created the Mandalorian?

    a) Henry Cavill
    b) Jon Favreau
    c) Sean Bean
    d) Quentin Tarantino

Answer: Pg. 81

29. What does Jar Jar Binks end up owing Qui-Gon for rescuing him?

a) A ship
b) A Bongo
c) An honor debt
d) A million credits

Answer: Pg. 81

30. Who is known as The Mandalorian?

a) Mai Saronah
b) Rood Bareesta
c) Din Djarin
d) Kah-ren Chumbawumpa

Answer: Pg. 81

31. What Broadway star composed music for Star Wars: The Force Awakens?

a) Andrew Lloyd Webber
b) Idina Menzel
c) Nick Cordero
d) Lin-Manuel Miranda

Answer: Pg. 81

32. What were Padmé's last words?

    a) "Obi-Wan... there... is good in him. I know there is."
    b) "Please, I'll give you anything. Anything you want!"
    c) "We're losing power. There seems to be a problem with
        the main reactor."
    d) "You were right, Obi-Wan."

Answer: Pg. 82

33. Which planet does the farmer Omera live on?

    a) Tatooine
    b) Sorgan
    c) Jakku
    d) Coruscant

Answer: Pg. 82

Category 5: Answers

Question	Letter	Answer
1	D	Don't Join
2	A	Anthony Daniels
3	C	Geonosis
4	B	His faith in his friends
5	B	Luke
6	C	Ducain
7	B	He lost his right arm
8	A	Bail Organa
9	C	"If you see our son, bring him home."
10	C	Tom Hardy
11	A	Raddus
12	B	Fathiers
13	C	Black Leader
14	B	In the remains of an AT-AT
15	D	Eight
16	A	"We all need to fight."
17	A	FN-2187
18	D	Hosnian
19	C	Daniel Radcliffe
20	A	Count Dooku
21	B	Princess Leia
22	C	Sanitation
23	B	Happabore
24	D	Temiri Blegg
25	B	AT-M6
26	C	60
27	A	Ahch-To
28	B	Jon Favreau
29	C	An honor debt
30	C	Din Djarin
31	D	Lin-Manuel Miranda

32	A	"Obi-Wan... there... is good in him. I know there is."
33	B	Sorgan

Category 6: Videogames

1. In Animal Crossing: New Horizons, other than Isabelle's daily announcements, where else can you get information about island events?

    a)   A message in a bottle
    b)   Tom Nook
    c)   The bulletin board
    d)   A letter from a villager

Answer: Pg. 95

2. In Rayman Legends, which Of These Is **NOT** A Level Painting?

    a)   Dungeon Dash
    b)   Armored Toad!
    c)   Cake Escape!
    d)   The Shaolin Master Dojo

Answer: Pg. 95

3. Which one of these songs isn't on SingStar Celebration's track list?

    a)   Britney Spears - Toxic-

b) Elle King - Ex's and Oh's
c) Fun. - Some Nights
d) Meghan Trainor - All About That Bass

Answer: Pg. 95

4. Which one of these isn't a recipe in Overcooked! 2

a) Sashimi
b) Burger
c) Christmas dessert
d) Moussaka

Answer: Pg. 95

5. What is the tagline for Pro Evolution Soccer 2016?

a) "The Season Starts Here"
b) "Love the Past, Play the Future"
c) "Where Legends are Made"
d) "Can you Play?"

Answer: Pg. 95

6. In Plants vs. Zombies: Battle for Neighborville, which is **not** an area in Weirding Woods?

a) Camp Near-a-Lake
b) Stirring Swamp
c) Z-Tech Factory
d) Steep Mines

Answer: Pg. 95

7, What is Cuphead's gameplay centered around?

a) Continual boss fighting
b) Continual running
c) Shoot and Run
d) Puzzle Solving

Answer: Pg. 95

8. FIFA 20 features three cover stars across all regional editions. Who is not one of the stars?

a) Zinedine Zidane
b) Eden Hazard
c) Kenny Dalglish
d) Virgil van Dijk

Answer: Pg. 95

9. In Crash Bandicoot N. Sane Trilogy, whose picture can you see in the cutscene of Crash Bandicoot 3 in Crash's house?

- a) Sephiroth from the Final Fantasy Series
- b) Nathan Drake from the Uncharted series
- c) Link from the Legend of Zelda series
- d) Super Mario

Answer: Pg. 95

10. In Ori and the Blind Forest, what creature is Ori?

- a) A faerie
- b) A wolf
- c) A guardian spirit
- d) An angel

Answer: Pg. 95

11. What was Sonic the Hedgehog originally going to be named?

- a) Flashhog
- b) Speedrun
- c) Lightnininghog
- d) Mr. Needlemouse

Answer: Pg. 95

12. How many levels are in Peggle 2?

a) 130 levels
b) 150 levels
c) 120 levels
d) 160 levels

Answer: Pg. 95

13. What's the name of the island in the middle of the Fortnite map?

a) Fort Isle
b) Eye Land
c) It doesn't have a name
d) Llama Island

Answer: Pg. 95

14. Which European city inspired Unravel's landscape?

a) Orimattila, Finland
b) Hruni, Iceland
c) Umeå, Sweden
d) Tromsø, Norway

Answer: Pg. 95

15. In Rocket League what crate can you get Draco Wheels from?

    a)   Accelerated Crate
    b)   Halloween Crate
    c)   Turbo Crate
    d)   Nitro Crate

Answer: Pg. 95

16. In the Pokémon Games which of these isn't a town in Kanto?

    a)   Chartreuse City
    b)   Viridian City
    c)   Fuchsia City
    d)   Cerulean City

Answer: Pg. 95

17. In Super Mario Odyssey what super useful powers does Cappy (Mario's hat) have?

    a)   It is invincible
    b)   Possess enemies and objects
    c)   Shoots fire
    d)   Summons a ship for Mario

Answer: Pg. 95

18. Which of these is NOT a dimension in Minecraft?

    a) The Nether
    b) The End
    c) The Overworld
    d) The Sideworld

Answer: Pg. 95

19. In Splatoon 2 What is the main goal when playing Turf War?

    a) Paint the floor.
    b) Paint the walls.
    c) Paint the walls AND the floor.
    d) Paint your opponents.

Answer: Pg. 95

20. Which of these Pokémon has both an Alolan and a Galarian form?

    a) Stunfisk
    b) Meowth
    c) Sandslash
    d) Ponyta

21. In Rayman Legends which Of These Is NOT A Playable
Character?

    a) Twila
    b) Olympia
    c) Athena
    d) Estelia

Answer: Pg. 95

22. Which was the first game in the Mario Kart series to include
open circuits.?

    a) Mario Kart 7
    b) Mario Kart DS
    c) Mario Kart Wii
    d) Mario Kart 8

Answer: Pg. 95

23. In Crash Team Racing, what color is Dingodile's car?

    a) Purple
    b) Lime
    c) Black
    d) Blue

Answer: Pg. 95

24. In Super Mario Party, what should you focus on in the Sound Stage mode?

    a)   The lights
    b)   Your opponent's controller
    c)   The rhythm
    d)   The colors

Answer: Pg. 95

25. In Overwatch, what is Tracer's girlfriend called?

    a)   Maria
    b)   Emma
    c)   Emily
    d)   Marisa

Answer: Pg. 96

26. In Crash Team Racing, which of the following weapons could not be used to open the short cut on the Tiger Temple race track?

    a)   Green Potion Bottle

b) Engine Boost
c) Missile
d) Nitro Crate

Answer: Pg. 96

27. What is the name of the level featured in every version of
Super Mario Kart?

a) Rainbow Road
b) Yellow-brick Road
c) Mushroom Road
d) Rocky Road

Answer: Pg. 96

28. NBA 2K is a series of basketball simulation games. Who is
the company currently publishing it?

a) Sega Sports
b) Nintendo Sports
c) Sony Sports
d) 2K Sports

Answer: Pg. 96

29. In Splatoon 2, which of these is not a weapon class?

a) Brellas
b) Shooters
c) Dynamoes
d) Dualies

Answer: Pg. 96

30. Which feature is new to Mario Party's mode?

a) Helpful allies
b) Character Dice Blocks
c) Shiny Coins
d) Super Stars

Answer: Pg. 96

31. In Animal Crossing New Horizons, what is Blathers afraid of?

a) Fish
b) Bugs
c) Fossils
d) Rain

Answer: Pg. 96

32. In Overwatch, who is Brigitte Lindholm's father?

94

a) Torbjörn
b) Reinhardt
c) Soldier 76
d) Reaper

Answer: Pg. 96

33. How many playable characters are there in Super Smash Bros?

a) 22
b) 30
c) 200+
d) 70+

Answer: Pg. 96

Category 6: Answers

Question	Letter	Answer
1	C	The bulletin board
2	C	Cake Escape!
3	A	Britney Spears – Toxic
4	D	Moussaka
5	B	"Love the Past, Play the Future"
6	D	Steep Mines
7	A	Kenny Dalglish. Eden Hazard was the cover star of the Regular Edition, Virgil van Dijk on the Champions Edition, and Zinedine Zidane on the Ultimate Edition.
8	C	Continual boss fighting
9	B	Nathan Drake from the Uncharted series
10	C	A guardian spirit
11	D	Mr. Needlemouse
12	C	120 levels
13	B	Eye Land
14	C	Umeå, Sweden
15	D	Nitro Crate
16	A	Chartreuse City
17	B	Possess enemies and objects
18	D	The Sideworld
19	A	Paint the floor. The score only counts the ground as inkable turf.
20	B	Meowth
21	C	Athena
22	A	Mario Kart 7
23	B	Lime. The purple car belongs to N. Gin and the black car belongs to Pinstripe. The blue car belongs to Crash.
24	C	The rhythm/The beat

25	C	Emily
26	B	Engine Boost. If you try going through this shortcut with it you will just ram into the wall.
27	A	Rainbow Road
28	D	2K Sports
29	C	Dynamoes. The Dynamo is in the Roller class.
30	B	Each character comes with their own special Dice Block that's made just for them.
31	B	He is afraid of bugs but still has to deal with them because of the museum.
32	A	Torbjörn
33	D	70+

Category 7: Books

1. In Cressida Cowell's "How to Train Your Dragon" this phrase is said:

    a)   "We killed dragons when I was a boy."
    b)   "There were dragons when I was a boy."
    c)   "There were no dragons when I was a boy."
    d)   "I saw dragons when I was a boy."

Answer: Pg. 110

2. In 'The Graveyard Book' by Neil Gaiman, what item did every member of Old Town receive on the day of the Macabre?

    a)   A white flower
    b)   A skull
    c)   A diamond
    d)   A piece of chocolate

Answer: Pg. 110

3. In Roald Dahl's "Matilda", what did Bruce Bogtrotter steal from Miss Trunchbull?

a) Ice Cream
b) Sour Patch Kids
c) Her money
d) A slice of chocolate cake

Answer: Pg. 110

4. In C.S. Lewis's "The Lion, the Witch and the Wardrobe", what type of candy does Edmund love above all else?

a) Mars
b) Butterfinger
c) Turkish Delight
d) Jolly Rancher

Answer: Pg. 110

5. In "Diary of a Wimpy Kid", what type of music does Rodrick like listening to?

a) Heavy Metal
b) Hip Hop
c) Christmas Music
d) Smooth Jazz

Answer: Pg. 110

6. In "A Series of Unfortunate Events" what do workers at Lucky Smells Lumbermill eat for lunch?

a) Walnuts
b) Peanuts
c) Spaghetti
d) Chewing Gum

Answer: Pg. 110

7. In "A Wrinkle in Time", what was the name of the planet where Meg's father was held captive?

a) Camazotz
b) Mars
c) Citagazze
d) Kit Kat

Answer: Pg. 110

8. In "Coraline", what is different about the people who were created by the other mother?

a) They only ate rats
b) They were younger
c) They had buttons for eyes
d) They were made of wax

Answer: Pg. 110

9. In "Artemis Fowl", what does Artemis give Holly to cure his mother from insanity?

a)   An acorn
b)   The Book of the People
c)   A promise to stop his criminal activities
d)   Half of his gold

Answer: Pg. 110

10. In Dahl's "Matilda", What did Mr. Wormwood rub into his hair every morning to keep it strong?

a)   Egg Hair mask
b)   Nutella
c)   Oil of violets hair tonic
d)   Oil of Possum hair tonic

Answer: Pg. 110

11. In "Anne of Green Gables", why does Anne start being scared of night journeys to Diana's house?

a) She learns the legend of a murderer
b) She imagines that the woods are haunted
c) She thinks Diana's mother is a vampire
d) She is afraid she will run into Gilbert?

Answer: Pg. 110

12. What were the names of Meg's twin brothers?

a) Mag and Mug
b) Charles and Wallace
c) Calvin and Hinky
d) Sandy and Dennys

Answer: Pg. 110

13. In "Aru Shah and the End of Time", how old is Aru Shah?

a) 12
b) 11
c) 13
d) 10

Answer: Pg. 110

14. In Rick Riordan's Percy Jackson universe, swearing on what river is the most serious oath you can make?

a) Lethe
b) Styx
c) Cocytus
d) Acheron

Answer: Pg. 110

15. In Cressida Cowell's "How to Train Your Dragon" series,
what is Hiccup's mother's name?

a) Big Boobied Bertha
b) Valka
c) Valhallarama
d) Astrid

Answer: Pg. 110

16. In the Artemis Fowl series, Captain Holly Short is a member
of what organization?

a) Lower Entertainment Patrol
b) Light Energy Provider
c) Lowly Elegant Pollutants
d) Lower Elements Police

Answer: Pg. 110

17. In "His Dark Materials" series, two angels help Will. What are their names?

a) Balthamos and Baruch
b) Enoch and Metatron
c) Gabriel and Gulliver
d) Michael and Raphael

Answer: Pg. 110

18. In "Coraline", how did Coraline get rid of the other mother entirely?

a) She burned her button eyes
b) She dropped an anvil on her
c) She threw the key to the door down the well and the hand of the other mother went down too
d) She locked her in the oven

Answer: Pg. 110

19. In Percy Jackson and the Olympians, what color food does Percy's mother always make him?

a) Purple
b) Blue
c) Green
d) Pink

Answer: Pg. 110

20. In Inkheart what was the first item Mo read out of a story?

    a) A white rabbit
    b) A red hooded cape
    c) A beanstalk
    d) A glass slipper

Answer: Pg. 110

21. In "Charlie and the Chocolate Factory", when Charlie gets
the change from his dollar bill, what does he do?

    a) He says goodbye and leaves
    b) He hides it to keep for himself
    c) He buys another chocolate bar and puts the rest away
        for his mother
    d) He spends the rest on more chocolate

Answer: Pg. 110

22. In Howl's Moving Castle, who are Sophie's sisters?

    a) Lettie and Betty

b) Martha and Bertha
c) Betty and Bertha
d) Lettie and Martha

Answer: Pg. 110

23. In "A Series of Unfortunate Events", what kind of cake does Uncle Monty serve the Baudelaires?

a) Carrot cake
b) Fruit Cake
c) Coconut Cream Cake
d) Chocolate Cake

Answer: Pg. 110

24. In "Doll Bones" what is the name of William the Blade's boat?

a) The Scallywag
b) Queen Anne's Revenge
c) The Titanic
d) Neptune's Pearl

Answer: Pg. 110

25 In "The Little Prince", why does the discovery of the rose garden make the little prince sad?

   a) He is allergic to roses
   b) He sees roses have thorns
   c) He realizes roses aren't only red
   d) He learns that his rose is not the only rose in the universe

Answer: Pg. 110

26. In "James and the Giant Peach", where do James and his new family live after the peach is gone?

   a) Inside the peach pit
   b) In James' aunts old house
   c) In a hot air balloon
   d) In a castle

Answer: Pg. 110

27. In "Charlie and the Chocolate Factory", what does Mr. Wonka urge the Indian Prince Pondicherry to do with his chocolate palace?

   a) Bury it
   b) Clean it properly
   c) Gift it to his wife

d) Eat it quickly

Answer: Pg. 111

28. In "His Dark Materials", what is Will Parry's daemon called?

a) Ciara
b) Zikri
c) Kirjava
d) Xeniamix

Answer: Pg. 111

29. In the Narnia books, what kind of money is used in Calormen?

a) Crescents
b) Doubloons
c) Suns
d) Denarius

Answer: Pg. 111

30. In the "Magnus Chase and the Gods of Asgard" series, who is Magnus's father?

a) Cornelius Chase

b) The Norse God Frey
c) Chevy Chase
d) The Norse God Odin

Answer: Pg. 111

31. Who gets abducted by aliens in "Fortunately, the milk"?

a) The brother
b) The sister
c) The dad
d) The mom

Answer: Pg. 111

32. Finish the quote from "Peter Pan and Wendy": "All children, except one, ___________."

a) Grow up
b) Can fly
c) Believe in fairies
d) Are pirates

Answer: Pg. 111

33. In "The Lion, the Witch and the Wardrobe", who are the four Pevensie children?

a) Peter, Edmund, Sophie, and Lily
b) Peter, Edmund, Susan, and Lucy
c) Paul, Edmund, Susan, and Lily
d) Peter, Edmund, Sophie, and Lucy

Answer: Pg. 111

Category 7: Answers

Question	Letter	Answer
1	B	"There were dragons when I was a boy."
2	A	A white flower
3	D	A slice of chocolate cake
4	C	Turkish Delight
5	A	Heavy Metal
6	D	Chewing Gum
7	A	Camazotz
8	C	They had buttons for eyes
9	D	Half of his gold
10	C	Oil of violets hair tonic
11	B	She imagines that the woods are haunted
12	D	Sandy and Dennys
13	A	12
14	B	The River Styx
15	C	Valhallarama
16	D	Lower Elements Police
17	A	Balthamos and Baruch
18	C	She threw the key to the door down the well and the hand of the other mother went down too
19	B	Blue
20	B	A red hooded cape
21	C	He buys another chocolate bar and puts the rest away for his mother
22	D	Lettie and Martha
23	C	Coconut Cream Cake
24	D	Neptune's Pearl
25	D	He learns that his rose is not the only rose in the universe
26	A	Inside the peach pit

27	D	Eat it quickly
28	C	Kirjava
29	A	Crescents
30	B	Magnus is the son of Frey, the Norse god of spring and summer.
31	C	The dad
32	A	Grow up
33	B	Peter, Edmund, Susan, and Lucy

Category 8: Disney

"Here is the world of imagination, hopes, and dreams."

- Walt Disney

1.What fictional country is Prince Naveen from?

   a) Malania
   b) Maldonia
   c) Caldonia
   d) Calzone

Answer: Pg. 125

2.When Nemo was put in a fish tank in "Finding Nemo", what new name did the other fish give him?

   a) Wormfood
   b) Rookie
   c) Bozo
   d) Sharkbait

Answer: Pg. 125

3.In Aladdin, what item did Jasmine steal from the marketplace?

   a) A rug
   b) An apple
   c) A loaf of bread
   d) A bracelet

Answer: Pg. 125

4.Which organization do Bernard and Miss Bianca work for in
"The Rescuers"?

   a) The Rescue Aid Society
   b) The Rescuers
   c) The Rescue Rangers
   d) The Rescuing Mice

Answer: Pg. 125

5.In "Lady and the Tramp," why does Jim give his wife Lady as a
gift?

   a) Because she has a new baby
   b) For her birthday
   c) For Christmas
   d) For their anniversary

Answer: Pg. 125

6.Who calls Jiminy Cricket a grasshopper in "Pinocchio"?

    a)   Pinocchio
    b)   Lampwick
    c)   The Blue Fairy
    d)   Stromboli

Answer: Pg. 125

7. To how many pups does Perdita gives birth to in the "101 Dalmatians"?

    a)   15
    b)   12
    c)   13
    d)   101

Answer: Pg. 125

8.Who has the first line in the movie "Tangled"?

    a)   Rapunzel
    b)   Flynn Rider
    c)   Mother Gothel
    d)   The Queen

Answer: Pg. 125

9.Who is the only Disney princess to have a tattoo?

   a) Ariel
   b) Belle
   c) Tiana
   d) Pocahontas

Answer: Pg. 125

10.Finish the lyrics to this song from "The Little Mermaid":
"Wouldn't you think I'm the girl, the girl who has everything?
Look at this trove, treasures untold..."

   a) "It's full of gizmos and gadgets galore."
   b) "Wonders from all over the world."
   c) "How many wonders can one cavern hold?"
   d) "What do you get to a girl who has everything?"

Answer: Pg. 125

11.Finish these "Frozen" lyrics: "My soul is spiraling in frozen
fractals all around..."

a) "And while my power feels hard like an icy blast"
b) "The cold is making me forget about the past."
c) "And though my people hate me it's all in the past."
d) "And one thought crystallizes like an icy blast."

Answer: Pg. 125

12. There are two Disney princesses who become royalty through marriage. Who are they?

a) Cinderella and Belle
b) Ariel and Belle
c) Snow White and Cinderella
d) Tiana and Ariel

Answer: Pg. 125

13.Mickey and Minnie Mouse used to have different names? What were they?

a) Mortimer and Minneola
b) Mortimer and Minerva
c) Michael and Milly
d) Mickelous and Minneola

Answer: Pg. 125

14. When Alice meets the White Rabbit, what is he holding apart from a pocket watch?

    a)   A potion bottle
    b)   A hat
    c)   A tea cup
    d)   An umbrella

Answer: Pg. 125

15. Who is Merlin's pet owl in "The Sword in the Stone"?

    a)   Aristotle
    b)   Homer
    c)   Herodotus
    d)   Archimedes

Answer: Pg. 125

16. How does Wendy first encounter Peter Pan?

    a)   Chasing his shadow around the bedroom
    b)   Trying to convince Tinkerbell to not harm Wendy
    c)   Trying to attach his shadow with soap
    d)   Hovering over her

Answer: Pg. 125

17. In "Sleeping Beauty," what do the fairies give to Prince
Phillip to fight Maleficent?

   a)   Sword of Destiny and Shield of Courage
   b)   Sword of Righteousness and Shield of Honor
   c)   Sword of Retribution and Shield of Triumph
   d)   Sword of Truth and Shield of Virtue

Answer: Pg. 125

18. In "Pocahontas," what did Pocahontas see in her dream that
made her believe that a change was coming?

   a)   A spinning arrow
   b)   A cloud made of flames
   c)   A hawk with red eyes
   d)   A burning door

Answer: Pg. 125

19.In "Sleeping Beauty," what is the name of Maleficent's pet
raven?

   a)   Malum
   b)   Mr. Horrible
   c)   Evil weevil

d) Diablo

Answer: Pg. 125

20. In "Frozen," how many brothers does Hans have?

   a) 9
   b) 12
   c) 15
   d) 11

Answer: Pg. 125

21. In "Beauty and the Beast," how many eggs does Gaston say he eats?

   a) Five dozen
   b) Four dozen
   c) Nine dozen
   d) Ten dozen

Answer: Pg. 125

22. In "Hercules," Hades promises not to harm Megara if Hercules gives up his strength for...?

   a) 12 hours

b) 36 hours
c) 24 hours
d) 48 hours

Answer: Pg. 125

23. In "Peter Pan," what did Captain Hook lose to the crocodile?

a) Left leg
b) Left hand
c) Right hand
d) Right leg

Answer: Pg. 125

24.In "The Little Mermaid," what name does Ursula use when she becomes human?

a) Alexia
b) Fallon
c) Olga
d) Vanessa

Answer: Pg. 125

25. Why is the Horned King searching for the Black Cauldron?

    a) It has the power to create an army of undead warriors
    b) It has the power to give him a new body
    c) It has the power to control all humans.
    d) It has the power to grant him any wish he wants

Answer: Pg. 125

26. What does the matchmaker criticize Mulan for?

    a) Being too tall
    b) Having bad breath
    c) Being too skinny
    d) Having bad teeth

Answer: Pg. 125

27.What's Simba's mother's name in the Lion King?

    a) Sarabi
    b) Nala
    c) Gekari
    d) Janelle

Answer: Pg. 125

28.What does the enchanted cake in "Brave" turn Merida's mother into?

   a) A seal
   b) A horse
   c) A bear
   d) A goat

Answer: Pg. 125

29.What is the name of the pub that Flynn brings Rapunzel to in "Tangled?"

   a) The Cuddly Bearcub
   b) The Purry Lion
   c) The Fuzzy Pupper
   d) The Snuggly Duckling

Answer: Pg. 126

30.What are the names of Ursula's eels?

   a) Flotsam and Jetsam
   b) Phobos and Tromos
   c) Bilge and Cod
   d) Callie and Murray

Answer: Pg. 126

31.What animal was Tarzan raised by?

- a) Gorillas
- b) Wolves
- c) Panthers
- d) Bears

Answer: Pg. 126

32.What's the name of Snow White's prince?

- a) Florian
- b) Phillip
- c) Eric
- d) Adam

Answer: Pg. 126

33. How many tentacles did Dory's octopus friend have in the movie Finding Dory?

- a) Seven
- b) Eight

c) Nine
d) Six

Answer: Pg. 126

Category 8: Answers

Question	Letter	Answer
1	B	Maldonia
2	D	Sharkbait
3	B	An apple
4	A	The Rescue Aid Society
5	C	For Christmas
6	B	Lampwick
7	A	15
8	B	Flynn Rider
9	D	Pocahontas
10	C	"How many wonders can one cavern hold?"
11	D	"And one thought crystallizes like an icy blast."
12	A	Cinderella and Belle
13	B	Mortimer and Minerva
14	D	An umbrella
15	D	Archimedes
16	C	She finds Peter Pan trying to attach his shadow with soap
17	D	Sword of Truth and Shield of Virtue
18	A	A spinning arrow
19	D	Diablo
20	B	12
21	A	Five dozen
22	C	24 hours
23	B	Left hand
24	D	Vanessa
25	A	It has the power to create an army of undead warriors
26	C	Being too skinny
27	A	Sarabi
28	C	A bear

29	D	The Snuggly Duckling
30	A	Flotsam and Jetsam
31	A	Gorillas
32	A	Florian
33	A	Seven

Category 9: Theme Parks

"In a way, it's nice to know that there are Greek gods out there, because you have somebody to blame when things go wrong."

- Percy Jackson

1. Where can you find the "Eejanaika" roller coaster that holds the world record for the most inversions?

    a) Tokyo Disneyland
    b) Toshimaen
    c) Fuji-Q Highland
    d) Hanayashiki

Answer: Pg. 140

2. How many water rides does Cedar Point have?

    a) None
    b) 1
    c) 5
    d) 2

Answer: Pg. 140

3. What is the oldest continually operating amusement park in the US?

    a) Cedar Point
    b) Lake Compounce
    c) Coney Island
    d) Six Flags

Answer: Pg. 140

4. What amusement park food was first seen at the 1904 Paris Exposition?

    a) Funnel cake
    b) Cotton candy
    c) Corn dog
    d) Pop corn

Answer: Pg. 140

5. What is the world's largest indoor theme park?

    a) Nickelodeon Universe
    b) Ferrari World

c) Warner Bros World Abu Dhabi
d) Galaxyland

Answer: Pg. 140

6.What is the oldest theme park in California?

a) Knott's Berry Farm
b) Six Flags Magic Mountain
c) California's Great America
d) Legoland

Answer: Pg. 140

7. Which is the UK's fastest rollercoaster, at 80mph?

a) Megafobia
b) The Ultimate
c) Mumbo Jumbo
d) Stealth

Answer: Pg. 140

8. Which Ferris wheel is the world's tallest?

a) High Roller, Las Vegas
b) Singapore Flyer
c) London Eye
d) Grand Roue de Paris

Answer: Pg. 140

9. Riding which ride at Disney World could help dislodge kidney stones?

a) Avatar Flight of Passage
b) Big Thunder Mountain Railroad
c) DINOSAUR
d) Kali River Rapids

Answer: Pg. 140

10. How old was the oldest person to ride a roller coaster?

a) 97
b) 120
c) 105
d) 85

Answer: Pg. 140

11. Great America opened in 1976. Which coaster was not open then?

    a) Gulf Coaster
    b) Willard's Whizzer
    c) Tidal Wave
    d) Turn of the Century

Answer: Pg. 140

12. In Sea World Orlando there is a giant roller coaster that goes into underground aquariums. What mythical creature is it named after?

    a) Loch Ness monster
    b) Kraken
    c) Scylla
    d) Jordmundgar

Answer: Pg. 140

13. In 2000, Blackpool Pleasure Beach opened a new ride which uses special effects, and thousands of gallons of water. What mythological place is it named after?

    a) Avalon
    b) Atlantis

c) Hades
d) Valhalla

Answer: Pg. 140

14. What else is a carousel known as?

a) Roller coaster
b) Merry-go-round
c) Tilt-A-Whirl
d) Horse spinner

Answer: Pg. 140

15. How many waterslides does 'Falls of Terror' in Lightwater Valley, North Yorkshire offer?

a) Three
b) Four
c) It's not a water ride
d) One

Answer: Pg. 141

16. What makes Knoebels Amusement Resort so popular?

a) It's open 24/7
b) Free admission
c) Free food
d) Free parking

Answer: Pg. 141

17. Which ride incorporates centrifugal force?

a) Carousel
b) Insanity
c) Drop Towers
d) Rotor

Answer: Pg. 141

18. Which park opened the first log ride, called the El Aserradero?

a) Six Flags Over Texas
b) Walt Disney World
c) Cedar Point, Sandusky, Ohio
d) Busch Gardens Tampa

Answer: Pg. 141

19. What material is used for the floor of the bumper car ride?

a) Wood
b) Concrete
c) Rubber
d) Graphite

Answer: Pg. 141

20. Which United States amusement park has a state line running through it?

a) Coney Island
b) Six Flags America
c) Carowinds
d) Navy Pier

Answer: Pg. 141

21. Who came up with the idea for the first Ferris wheel?

a) Allan Herschell
b) George Washington Gale Ferris Jr.
c) Ernst Hoffmeister
d) Chance Morgan

Answer: Pg. 141

22. To get your thrills on the Insanity, you will have to go where?

   a) New York
   b) Las Angeles
   c) Las Vegas
   d) Orlando

Answer: Pg. 141

23. Which amusement park holds the world record for the number of rides featured?

   a) Cedar Point
   b) Coney Island
   c) Walt Disney World
   d) Six Flags America

Answer: Pg. 141

24. Where did Herbert Sellner construct his very first Tilt-A-Whirl?

   a) His neighborhood's stadium
   b) Chicago World's Fair
   c) Disneyland
   d) His own backyard

Answer: Pg. 141

25. What is Kings Dominion's slogan?

    a)   I'm Loving It
    b)   It's Amazing in Here
    c)   The Greatest Fun in A Million Years
    d)   The Best Park in The World

Answer: Pg. 141

26. How do they do the ballroom scene in Disney's Haunted Mansion?

    a)   Phantasmagoria
    b)   Ambiguous Image
    c)   Troxler's Effect
    d)   Digital Projectors

Answer: Pg. 141

27. How much was the opening day admission at the Disney World's Magic Kingdom?

    a) $9
    b) $15
    c) $3.50

d) $1

Answer: Pg. 141

28. How many cars are attached to the Tilt-A-Whirl?

a) Ten
b) Seven
c) Nine
d) Thirteen

Answer: Pg. 141

29. Where can you find the oldest amusement park in the world?

a) Eskilstuna, Sweden
b) Munich, Germany
c) Vienna, Austria
d) Klampenborg, Denmark

Answer: Pg. 141

30. Why were carousel rides created?

a)   to train French nobles for equestrian events
b)   to help parents avoid buying ponies for children
c)   to practice for betting on horses at the track
d)   to train French soldiers for horse riding

Answer: Pg. 141

31. In 2007, the Log Flume Lake at Blackpool Pleasure Beach
was drained to accommodate a new ride. What did the workers
find after all the water was gone?

a)   A human skull
b)   Gold bars
c)   Marlene Dietrich's lost earring
d)   A family of alligators

Answer: Pg. 142

32. Which item is banned in ALL Disney theme parks?

a)   Suitcases
b)   Selfie Sticks
c)   Branded Clothing
d)   Glasses

Answer: Pg. 142

33. In Disney's Hollywood Studio, how long does it take Rock 'n' Roller Coaster to accelerate from 0 to 57 mph?

   a) 2.8 seconds
   b) 3.5 seconds
   c) 1.7 seconds
   d) 5 seconds

Answer: Pg. 142

Category 9: Answers

Question	Letter	Answer
1	C	In Fuji-Q Highland. This ride has a whopping 14 inversions! The name means "ain't it great?" in Japanese
2	D	Two
3	B	Lake Compounce in Bristol, CT is the oldest continuously operating park in the US. It opened in 1846
4	B	Machine-spun cotton candy was invented in 1897 by dentist William Morrison and confectioner John C. Wharton. It was first introduced to a wide audience at the 1904 World's Fair as "Fairy Floss"
5	C	Warner Bros World Abu Dhabi in the UAE spans an area of 1.65 million square feet.
6	A	Knott's Berry Farm, the oldest and one of the largest theme parks in the United States.
7	D	Stealth
8	A	High Roller, Las Vegas
9	B	Big Thunder Mountain Railroad
10	C	105-year old Jack Reynolds became the oldest person to ride a roller coaster. He broke the record at a theme park in England.
11	C	The Tidal Wave did not debut until the 1978
12	B	Kraken
13	D	Valhalla
14	B	Merry-go-round
15	A	Three, two of which require 1.1m of

		height instead of 1m
16	B	Free admission
17	D	The Rotor makes people stick to the walls by centrifugal force
18	A	In 1963, Six Flags Over Texas debuted the first ever log flume. El Aserradero, which is Spanish for "the sawmill".
19	D	The bumper car ride uses graphite flooring, which decreases the friction.
20	C	Carowinds sits on the line between North Carolina and South Carolina.
21	B	George (Washington Gale) Ferris Jr.
22	C	The Insanity is located in Las Vegas on the top of the Stratosphere Hotel Tower.
23	A	Cedar Point wins with 72 rides!
24	D	The first Tilt-A-Whirl was constructed in Sellner's backyard.
25	B	It's Amazing in Here
26	A	Phantasmagoria. The ghosts that appear and disappear in the **ballroom** below **you** are created using a projection technique known as phantasmagoria that dates back to the mid-1800s.
27	C	$3. 50
28	B	Seven
29	D	Dyrehavsbakken ("The Deer Pasture's Hill"), Bakken for short, the oldest amusement park on Earth, opened in 1583 in Denmark and still operates today.
30	A	Carousels came about in the 1600s, and were designed to help French noblemen practice for equestrian competitions

31	C	Marlene Dietrich's lost earring. After being invited to Pleasure Beach in 1934, Marlene Dietrich lost her earring after riding on the "Big Dipper". The earring was reported to have remained in excellent condition and was confirmed to be the actress' soon after discovery. Apart from the earring these items were also found: £85 in change, a bra, a toupee, 3 dolls, 3 sets of false teeth, and even a glass eye!
32	B	Selfie Sticks
33	A	2.8 seconds

Category 10: TV Shows

1. In 'My Little Pony: Friendship Is Magic', which pony dreams of joining the Wonderbolts?

    a)   Twilight Sparkle
    b)   Rainbow Dash
    c)   Pinkie Pie
    d)   Rarity

Answer: Pg. 156

2. What is Daffy Duck's "catchphrase"?

    a)   That's all folks!
    b)   You're despicable!
    c)   What's up, doc?
    d)   I did see a pussycat!

Answer: Pg. 156

3. In "Gravity Falls", Dipper has a birthmark in what shape?

    a)   A spoon

b) A star
c) A cockroach
d) The big Dipper

Answer: Pg. 156

4. In "Avatar: the last Airbender", whose girlfriend turned into the moon?

a) Sokka's
b) Zuko's
c) Aang's
d) Jet's

Answer: Pg. 156

5. What is the name of the cartoon created by Guillermo del Toro for Netflix?

a) Monsterhunters
b) Robothunters
c) Trollhunters
d) Kaijuhunters

Answer: Pg. 156

6. In "She-Ra and the Princesses of Power" who of these is not one of She-Ra's enemies?

   a) Shadow Weaver
   b) Catra
   c) Hordak
   d) Battle Cat

Answer: Pg. 156

7. Who is the leader of the Teen Titans in "Teen Titans, Go!"?

   a) Starfire
   b) Robin
   c) Raven
   d) Cyborg

Answer: Pg. 156

8. In "Steven Universe", who gave Pink Diamond the idea to become Rose Quartz?

   a) Ruby
   b) Sapphire
   c) Zircon
   d) Pearl

Answer: Pg. 156

9. In 'My Little Pony: Friendship Is Magic', who is Twilight Sparkle's mentor?

    a) Queen Nebula
    b) Discordia
    c) Princess Celestia
    d) Countess Dawnlight

Answer: Pg. 156

10. What color shirt does Theodore wear in "Alvin and the Chipmunks"?

    a) Red
    b) Blue
    c) Yellow
    d) Green

Answer: Pg. 156

11. Which of the following nicknames is Harumi also known as in "Lego Ninjago"?

    a) The Quiet One

b) The Chatty One
c) The Chosen One
d) The Happy One

Answer: Pg. 156

12. In the United Kingdom, the BBC broadcasts the series "Doctor Who." Which U.S. network first aired the new series?

a) FX
b) TNT
c) CW
d) Syfy

Answer: Pg. 156

13.What weird food does Schwoz like eating in "Henry Danger"?

a) Paper napkins
b) Worms
c) Pencil Shavings
d) Spiders

Answer: Pg. 156

14.Which planet does the Doctor come from in the series "Doctor Who"?

a) Gallifrey
b) Future Earth
c) Earth
d) Agora

Answer: Pg. 156

15. "Winx Club" follows the adventures of a group of girls known as the Winx, students in what college?

a) Wingamabob College for Witches
b) Allathea College of Beings
c) Alfea College for Fairies
d) Winxton College for Magical Creatures

Answer: Pg. 156

16.What symbol is on SpongeBob SquarePants' Krusty Krab hat?

a) A smiley face
b) A crab
c) The letters KK
d) A small blue anchor

Answer: Pg. 156

17. In "Avatar: the last Airbender", what was the name of Zuko's grandfather?

a) Azulon
b) Iroh
c) Ozai
d) Bumi

Answer: Pg. 156

18.Who is not a member of the Teen Titans in "Teen Titans, Go!"?

a) Raven
b) Beast Boy
c) Jinx
d) Robin

Answer: Pg. 156

19. Who is Sapphire's wife in "Steven Universe"?

a) Ruby
b) Opal
c) Topaz
d) Emerald

Answer: Pg. 156

20. What headband color isn't worn by any of the Teenage Mutant Ninja Turtles?

    a) Red
    b) Orange
    c) Blue
    d) Green

Answer: Pg. 156

21. In the TV show 'Catdog' what are Dog's favorite foods?

    a) Hot dogs with ketchup
    b) Fish with tartar sauce
    c) Tacos with hot sauce
    d) Vegetables with cheese sauce

Answer: Pg. 156

22. What is the country of origin of the animated series Rabbids Invasion?

    a) Canada

b) France
c) Belgium
d) Korea

Answer: Pg. 156

23.What instrument does Marceline play in "Adventure Time"?

a) Bass guitar
b) Flute
c) Violin
d) Drums

Answer: Pg. 156

24.What's Ice King's real name?

a) Simon
b) Steven
c) Adam
d) George

Answer: Pg. 157

25.In "Pig Goat Banana Cricket", who is obsessed with pickles?

a) Pig
b) Goat
c) Banana
d) Cricket

Answer: Pg. 157

26. In the "Legend of Korra", how are Mako and Bolin related?

a) Father and son
b) Cousins
c) They're not related
d) Brothers

Answer: Pg. 157

27. In "Trollhunters", what color is Jim´s amulet of daylight?

a) Yellow
b) Red
c) Blue
d) Orange

Answer: Pg. 157

28.The "Fairly OddParents" follows Timmy Turner, a 10-year-old boy with two fairy godparents named what?

a) Zumbo and Rachel
b) Shimmer and Shine
c) Cosmo and Wanda
d) Gizmo and Amanda

Answer: Pg. 157

29. What are SpongeBob SquarePants' parents called?

a) Henry SquarePants and Mary BubbleBottom
b) Harold SquarePants and Margaret BubbleBottom
c) Hector SquarePants and Millie BubbleBottom
d) Harry SquarePants and Martha BubbleBottom

Answer: Pg. 157

30. In "Gravity Falls", what is the name of Mabel's pig?

a) Hambone
b) Hamilton
c) Hamlet
d) Waddles

Answer: Pg. 157

31. What item is used to restore a wounded Z fighter to full health?

a) Z Sword
b) Saiyan hair
c) Capsule Corp medicine
d) Senzu bean

Answer: Pg. 157

32. In "The Wild Thornberrys", Eliza Thornberry has a special secret. What is it?

a) she can become invisible
b) she can talk to animals
c) she can become a snake
d) she can fly

Answer: Pg. 157

33. In the "Legend of Korra", what is Toph's second daughter's name?

a) Asami
b) Opal
c) Suyin
d) Lin

Answer: Pg. 157

Category 10: Answers

Question	Letter	Answer
1	B	Rainbow Dash
2	B	You're despicable! Daffy always speaks with a lisp, so it would actually be "You're desthpicable."
3	D	The big Dipper
4	A	Sokka's. That's rough, buddy!
5	C	Trollhunters: Tales of Arcadia
6	D	Battle Cat is He Man's animal companion.
7	B	Robin
8	D	Pearl. As Rose Quartz, Pink hid her true nature from everyone except Pearl, the one who originally suggested she take on the form of a Rose Quartz to begin with.
9	C	Princess Celestia
10	D	Green. Alvin wears red, Simon wears blue, and Theodore wears green.
11	A	The Quiet One
12	D	Syfy
13	B	Worms
14	A	The Doctor is a Time Lord from the planet Gallifrey.
15	C	Alfea College for Fairies
16	D	A small blue anchor
17	A	Azulon
18	C	Jinx
19	A	Ruby
20	D	Green
21	C	tacos with hot sauce
22	B	French
23	A	Bass guitar

24	A	Simon
25	A	Pig. Goat has musical dreams, Banana loves video games, and Cricket is talented at mad science.
26	D	They are brothers
27	C	Blue
28	C	Cosmo and Wanda
29	B	Harold SquarePants and Margaret BubbleBottom
30	D	Waddles
31	D	Senzu bean
32	B	She can talk to animals
33	C	Suyin

Bonus Questions!

We did promise you 333 questions and if you know your math ten times 33 equals only 330! So here are the rest!

331. Which DC superhero was Marvel's Deadpool borrowed from?

    a)   Wade Wilson
    b)   Slade Wilson
    c)   Glade Wilson
    d)   Blade Wilson

332. Who wrote Artemis Fowl?

    a)   Owen Wilson
    b)   Eoin Colfer
    c)   Eowyn Wilson
    d)   Eimhir Colfer

333. Who played Detective Pikachu?

    a)   Ryan Reynolds
    b)   Ryan Gosling
    c)   Ryan Wilson
    d)   Ryan Lochte

SPECIAL BONUS!

Want These 2 Bonus Books for <u>free</u>?

Get <u>FREE</u>, unlimited access to these and all of our new books by joining the KidsVille Books Facebook group!

PLUS! Get entered into our monthly $20 Amazon Gift card Giveaway

Conclusion

That's it! You made it all the way through 333 questions about everything from Avatar to the Zinedine Zidane. How do you feel? Did you learn something new? Did your friends?

These categories and questions were picked out especially for the kids and teens reading this book because entertainment is important for a great upbringing! All work and no play and all that! What other topics can you think of that might be fun for this kind of quiz? Maybe leave us some suggestions in your review – or even come up with some questions of your own!

Our team has been really excited throughout making this book, and we hope we excited and inspired you too. We look forward to seeing you join us in our next trivia adventure.

The End

(Nearly)

Reviews are not easy to come by.

As an independent author with a tiny marketing budget, I rely on readers, like you, to leave a short review on Amazon.

Even if it's just a sentence or two!